Nature Upclose

A Dandelion's Life

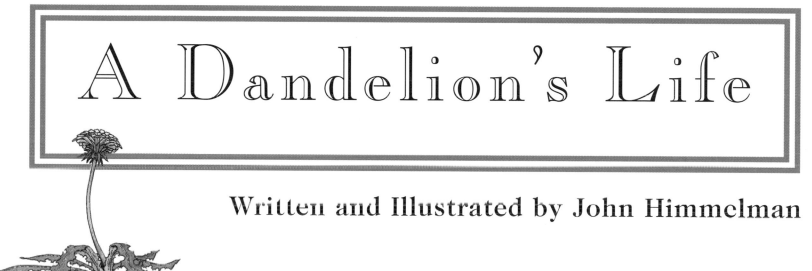

Written and Illustrated by John Himmelman

Children's Press®
A Division of Grolier Publishing

New York London Hong Kong Sydney
Danbury, Connecticut

For my editor, Melissa Stewart, whose guidance in this series has made it possible for you to be holding this book

Library of Congress Cataloging-in-Publication Data

Himmelman, John
   A dandelion's life / written and illustrated by John Himmelman.
      p.   cm. — (Nature upclose)
   Summary: Text and illustrations follow the life cycle of a dandelion, describing its germination, the growth of its flower head, visits by various insects, and the withering if its stem in winter.
      ISBN 0-516-21177-3 (lib. bdg.)   0-516-26402-8 (pbk.)
      1. Dandelion—Juvenile literature.   2. Dandelions—Life cycles—Juvenile literature.   [1. Dandelions.] I. Title.
II. Series: Himmelman, John. Nature upclose.
QK495.C74H55   1998
583'.99—dc21   97-31737
                                         CIP
                                         AC

Visit Children's Press on the Internet at:
   http://publishing.grolier.com

Common dandelion
Taraxacum officinale

You may be surprised to hear that a single dandelion flower head is made up of many small flowers. Most other plant buds develop into a single flower. When you look at a tulip or a violet or a lily flower, you are looking at a single flower. Some plants, such as dandelions, have what is called composite flowers. Many flowers bloom from a single flower head. Other examples of composite flowers include carnations, marigolds, and chrysanthemums.

Many people think of dandelions as weeds. The wind often drops their seeds on our lawns. Soon, yellow flower heads appear everywhere. Surprisingly, at one time, there were no dandelions in North America. The first seeds were accidentally brought to the Americas on the fur of stowaway rats or on the pants of sailors.

In late summer, a dandelion seed floats through the air.

434

It hitches a ride in a chipmunk's fur.

The seed drops into the *soil.*

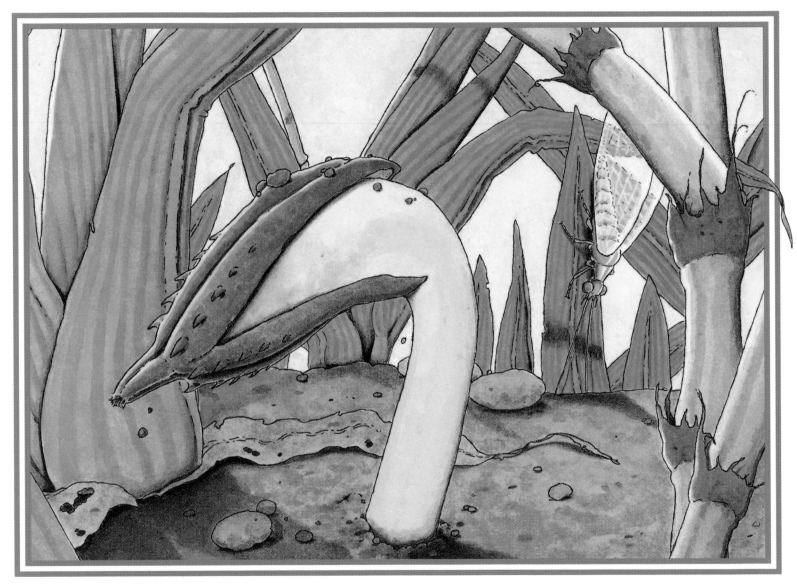

A few weeks later, a dandelion plant begins to *sprout.*

Its leaves grow and spread during the fall.

In winter, snow covers the dandelion and other plants. It is hard for birds to find food.

A *redpoll* eats grass seeds. Below the snow, the dandelion's leaves stay green all winter.

Spring rain waters thirsty roots.

In early summer, a stem grows up and a dandelion *bud* forms.

Soon, the bud opens and a bright yellow flower head appears.
The head contains dozens of little flowers.

A *skipper* visits the dandelion flowers for *nectar*.

The skipper will not fight with a wasp. It flies away.

In late afternoon, the flower head closes.

At night, a cricket comes out from under the dandelion's leaves.

It fills the warm summer evening with music.

As the sun rises, the dandelion flower head opens again.

A lawn mower roars across the yard!

Luckily, it just misses the dandelion.

The dandelion has many visitors. They all like its nectar.

Sometimes many visitors come at once.

A few days later, the flower head closes for the last time.

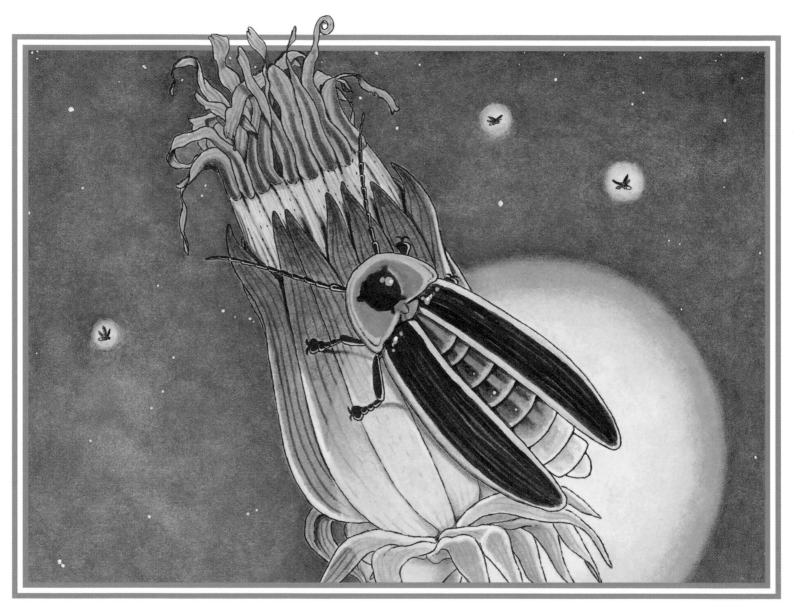

The dead flowers are slowly pushed out of the head.

They are replaced by a fuzzy ball of seeds.

The summer breeze lifts the dry, light seeds into the air.

Now the dandelion head is bare.

The stem withers, but the leaves keep growing. The plant will bud again next spring.

There will be many more seasons of dandelion flowers.

And many more seasons of seeds in the air.

Words You Know

bud—the part of a plant that turns into leaves, flowers, or roots.

nectar—a sweet liquid made by flowers that certain insects like to drink.

redpoll—a finch that likes snow-covered fields of weeds.

skipper—a small butterfly.

soil—the layers of dead plant matter and dirt that cover the ground.

sprout—to begin to grow.

About the Author

John Himmelman has written or illustrated more than forty books for children, including *Ibis: A True Whale Story*, *Wanted: Perfect Parents*, and *J.J. Versus the Babysitter*. His books have received honors such as Pick of the List, Book of the Month, JLG Selection, and the ABC Award. He is also a naturalist who enjoys turning over dead logs, crawling through grass, kneeling over puddles, and gazing at the sky. His greatest joy is sharing these experiences with others. John lives in Killingworth, Connecticut, with his wife Betsy who is an art teacher. They have two children, Jeff and Liz.